"*47 Secret Veterans' Benefits for Seniors* is a long overdue spotlight focusing on what millions of veterans don't even know they are missing out on. Victoria is to be applauded for leading the way in educating the Elder Law profession and Veterans about untapped financial resources and VA benefits that all too often go unclaimed. Benefits that can dramatically impact the level of care to be afforded.

This book will be instrumental in insuring a quality of life for those who defend our freedoms and make the sacrifice of service. Well written, informative, and should be on the desk of anyone dealing with Eldercare issues and should be in the home of every veteran."

—*Debbie Burak, Founder-VeteranAid.org, CEO-Woven Embrace.com*

VeteranAid.org was created by Ms Burak in 2005 with the mission of bringing the Improved Pension to National attention making it as common knowledge as Social Security, Medicare and Medicaid. VeteranAid.org is the most respected online resource on the topic of the VA's Aid and Attendance Pension Benefit and is ranked #1 nationally. She is respected throughout the Eldercare industry for her tireless efforts acting as a Veteran's Advocate, and is currently working with Congressional representatives to rewrite legislation that will help allow veterans better access to entitlements and benefits. As the daughter of a WWII veteran who discovered the pension at the passing of her father, Ms Burak made a promise to her mother to change the ending for others. That promise has been kept and has indeed changed the lives of thousands of grateful sons, daughters, and loved ones. Ms Burak is also the CEO of WovenEmbrace.com a sympathy and condolence gift site.

"I'm a Vietnam era American Army veteran. I'm proud of my service to my country. I suffered injuries while on active duty. As these injuries worsened over time, I took full advantage of my VA benefits.

Gaining those benefits isn't always easy. Even for a younger veteran who has the energy to confront the bureaucracy and the miles of red tape, VA is intimidating.

My service connected injuries forced me out of my long career in health care. As I retired, many friends were veterans and I helped them apply for their VA benefits. I decided to try to put it all into a format that made sense for others. I met Larry Scott, the founder and editor of the most popular veterans site on the Internet, www.VAWatchdog.org. To my surprise, Larry thought I had something to offer his readers and offered me a place in his organization.

Today I write a Question and Answer column for veterans, I opine editorially on occasion and I speak at veteran's events. I work with lawyers across the country to promote the simple idea that veterans who served honorably should receive all that is owed them. I maintain web sites to teach veterans how to navigate the VA system and I host a forum where vets may exchange advice and stories of "been there, done that."

Most of my work focuses on the average veteran. My readers are usually below the age of 65 or so. Many of my followers today are very young as the ongoing war on terror is giving us new generations of veterans.

The elderly veteran is often forgotten. These members of "The Greatest Generation" often suffer in silence or they may not know how to access the benefits they've earned.

Thankfully, Victoria Collier, Esq. has brought together knowledge and experience and she directly addresses the needs of this special group of veterans. Her work is timely as more of us are living longer and more productive lives. The overall numbers of veterans who are seniors with particular needs is significant and growing.

Victoria's direct and no-nonsense approach is perfect. Her "secrets"are easy to understand, accurate to a fault and relevant. This is a book every veteran who is approaching their senior years must read.

Veterans advocates and veterans family members should also take advantage of this opportunity to learn about benefits they never knew existed.

I'll be recommending it to my younger readers as well as older veterans.

These 47 Secrets aren't only for seniors, they're for every savvy veteran who wants to plan for their future.

This book is too good to be kept secret any longer!"

—*Jim Strickland*, *Author of The A to Z Guide to VA Disability Benefits,*
jimstrickland912.com

"As a VA accredited agent, co-founder of Veterans Advocates Group of America, and daughter of a veteran, I am well aware of the great difficulties that families face in navigating the Veterans Benefits system. As a nurse care manager who has personally helped over one thousand families over the last few years understand the VA claim process, I was thrilled to see that Victoria has written a book to help our deserving veterans and their dependents get the money that is rightfully owed to them. As someone who has known Victoria for many years, I believe that her unsurpassed knowledge related to VA made her the perfect choice to write this kind of book.

Victoria's book explains in simple language the benefits that are available and the criteria for each. Her approach is one that is not only caring, but without the legal jargon that is oftentimes so difficult for many people to understand. I have full confidence that anyone who reads this book will agree that it is one of the most important books ever written about VA.

I wish Victoria and all of our veterans and their families the very best this world has to offer."

—*Karen B. McIntyre*, *R.N. and VA Accredited Agent*

"Many disabled veterans and their widows walk in a desert of despair — plagued by the poor health and little or no money. Victoria Collier, Esq is a deep pool of compassion, knowledge and integrity that she uses to bring these American Hero's into the oasis of security."

—*Kenneth R. Clark*, *CPCU, CLTC, Certified Senior Advisor, Canton, GA*

In 26 years of elder law practice, effectively advising and advocating for veteran clients regarding Department of Veterans Administration benefits has been far more difficult than Medicaid planning partly because DVA has prevented individual lawyers from charging a reasonable fee. Few attorneys have been able to learn the rules as a result. Attorney Victoria Collier's experience as a military veteran and attorney for countless veterans have been distilled and creatively presented in her book *47 Secret Veterans' Benefits for Seniors*.

Rather than presenting V.A. advocacy strategies in the usual statutory citation method of similar works, she organizes her work based on ultimate outcomes that are intuitive, easy to understand and nicely prioritized. My learning process went from zero to 100 miles per hour almost instantly with better retention than my previous study of the complicated, horribly difficult maze of authority and procedure required for obtaining V.A. benefits.

If your practice includes advising elderly veterans and their families, Victoria's monumental work should be on your desk. Her seminars on V.A. benefits are as useful as this book. I highly recommend both.

*—**Tim Nay**, MSW, Attorney at Law, Captain, U.S.A.F.*
Founding President and Fellow,
National Academy of Elder Law Attorneys.

On the Cover

Veteran, Joseph McCabe, a client of Victoria Collier, commemorating the lives of veterans who have passed away, Veteran's Day Memorial Service at the Decatur, GA cemetery, November 11, 2009. Mr. McCabe served honorably in the US Navy. Below is a short biography taken from his diary.

Joe McCabe was born February 18, 1918, during the Spanish Flu Pandemic in New Orleans, Louisiana. In 1937, he joined the Naval Reserve and made annual training cruises in the Caribbean aboard WWI Destroyers. In April 1941, his unit was called to Active Duty and he reported to the U.S. Naval Training Center in San Diego.

While there he was selected, with a group, for background in the movie Navy Blues starring Ann Sheridan and Jack Okey. This film was also used at the founding of the U.S.O. at the Hollywood Bowl.

McCabe was sent to Miami, Florida, to pick up the yacht "Caroline" donated by the Duke of Windsor. It was converted to salvage crashed training aircraft and rescue trainees, from the Corpus Christi Naval Base.

He was transferred to the Brookland Navy Yard and assigned to the USS Monitor LSV-5 that carried amphibious tanks for use in the Pacific

Operation. It delivered tanks and troops to the many Pacific islands and participated in the battle to liberate the Philippines. The Monitor went on to a staging area called "Point Look" for assembling an armada of ships for the invasion of Japan.

On August 30th 1945, McCabe and the Monitor docked at Yokohama, Japan. He could see the USS Missouri, where the surrender ceremony was to be conducted.

Joe McCabe was discharged in November 1945. However, he was recalled to Active Duty in 1951, for the Korean War. He served as an instructor at Bainbridge Naval Station Maryland.

Joseph McCabe, Chief Quartermaster is currently Chaplain of the American Legion Post 66, Avondale Estates, Georgia.

47 Secret Veterans' Benefits for Seniors

47 SECRET VETERANS' BENEFITS
for Seniors

Benefits You Have EARNED...
...but Don't Know About!

Victoria L. Collier, JD

Veteran helping other Veterans

Published by Collier Communications, LLC

Published by
Collier Communications, LLC
Scottdale, GA 30079
www.colliercommunicationsllc.com

Publisher's Cataloging-in-Publication data

Collier, Victoria L.
    47 secret veterans' benefits for seniors : benefits you have earned ...but don't know about! / Victoria L. Collier, JD.
        p. cm.
        ISBN 978-0-9843949-0-6
1. Veterans --United States --Finance, Personal. 2. United States --Armed Forces --Pay, allowances, etc. 3. United States. Veterans Benefits Administration --Rules and practice. 4. Military pensions --United States. 5. Older people --Services for --United States. 6. Older people --Finance, Personal. I. Forty-seven veterans' benefits for seniors : benefits you have earned...but don't know about! II. Title.

UC74 .C65 2010
331.2/8135500973--dc22
    2010921734

Printed in the United States

ISBN: 978-0-9667970-4-6

Book and cover design by TH Design, LLC www.thdesign.com

★ ★ ★   ★ ★ ★

Table of Contents

Dedication

This book is dedicated to the service men and women with whom I served in the United States Air Force and United States Army Reserves, for helping me become who I am. Specifically, I would like to recognize Major Joseph Hyman, Master Sergeant Dianne Scheetz, Master Sergeant Tommy Turner, Staff Sergeant Timothy McVey (not the Oklahoma bomber), Staff Sergeant Mark deLong, Staff Sergeant Lou Powell, and Staff Sergeant Ellen Serdock, with whom I served in the Air Force. I would like to recognize Colonel Curtis Boren, Colonel Paul Laymon, Captain Lesli Seta, and Master Sergeant Brenda Hain, with whom I served in the Army Reserves.

Additionally, I would like to extend a special thank you to all persons who have served and supported our military forces throughout the years. Our country is what it is today because of the brave service of others.

I acknowledge that many veterans, such as myself, are female. However, for simplicity, I have primarily referenced veterans in this book as male. It is not my intention to offend anyone by my use of the male gender when referencing veterans in general.

Introduction

I am Victoria Collier and I am a veteran of the United States Air Force (1989-1995) and the United States Army Reserve (2001-2004). I joined the military when I was 19 years old. There are many different reasons why people join the military. Some want to follow in the footsteps of their fathers or grandfathers; some want to get out of their hometown and travel the world; some want to learn a trade or profession; some were involuntarily drafted. I joined because I moved out of my parents' house when I was 17 years old, still in high school. After graduation from high school, I worked hard – too hard, and at a rate of pay that was too low. I knew that I wanted more out of life. I also knew I was going nowhere fast.

So, after a year-and-a-half of working minimum wage at fast-food restaurants, retail clothing stores, and nursing homes, I knew I needed to do something else quickly. I contacted a recruiter, took the Armed Forces Vocational Aptitude Battery (ASVAB) test, and signed on the dotted line.

Enlisting in the Air Force was the best decision I have ever made.

Since then, I have become a lawyer, specializing in assisting senior citizens and veterans. I am accredited through the Veterans Administration (a special designation for individuals who want to assist veterans with their claims before the VA). I am admitted to practice before the United States Supreme Court and the United States Court of Veterans Claims. I am a member of numerous professional organizations, including the National Organization of Veteran Advocates and the National Academy of Elder Law Attorneys.

Because of my specialized experience and knowledge of veterans' benefits and senior citizen issues, I developed a training course for lawyers who want to help veterans. However, I felt it was important to reach out to you, the veteran, as well. I recognize that not everyone is comfortable consulting a lawyer. So, I wrote this book for you — veterans and family members of veterans. This book is designed specifically with the Senior Citizen Veteran in mind. It is my goal that you will have the knowledge you need about the most beneficial veterans' benefits available to senior citizens.

Why are we discussing veterans' benefits?

The reason I want to spread the word about veterans' benefits to as many people as I can is because of the positive impact it has on my clients and their lives. Not only do my clients have access to health care benefits they didn't previously know about, but most of them find they are also eligible for additional income through the VA to help pay for health care costs.

When a person is retired and living on a fixed income, preservation of resources becomes paramount. When health care costs begin to eat away at those resources, it can jeopardize the level of care a person receives as well as the family's life style, and can quickly impoverish the family. In today's environment, other forms of government assistance, such as Medicaid, are becoming more difficult to obtain. They are generally not available to people living at home or in an assisted living facility (certain exceptions apply in some states).

The Numbers

As of August 3, 2009, the projected number of living

veterans in the U.S. was 23,442,000. Of those, 39.4% (9,236,148) are 65 years of age or older. The projected number of living World War II veterans as of September 30, 2008, was 2,583,000. Additionally, there are many more living, elderly veterans who served in other war- time periods.

As of August 3, 2009, **3.03 million** veterans were receiving service connected disability compensation, with 273,300 of them rated as 100% disabled. At that time, there were 312,669 veterans receiving pensions and 323,189 widowed spouses receiving death indemnity compensation. If you are unfamiliar with all the terms I am using, don't worry — just keep reading and you will learn them.

Part I – Basic Training: Preliminary Information You Should Know

Veterans Benefits are Not New

This book will discuss certain VA benefits that are most beneficial to senior citizens, specifically, VA service connected compensation, VA health care, and VA pension benefits. The first U.S. Congress passed a law in 1789 to provide pensions to disabled veterans and their dependents. A lot happened between 1789 and 1930, but in 1930 the Veterans Administration (VA) was established to consolidate and coordinate government activity affecting war veterans. Our country has a long history of protecting those people who have gone to war to protect our rights. The VA experienced enormous growth after World War II when 16 million veterans returned home. This led to the creation of the Department of Veterans Benefits in 1953, to administer the VA's huge compensation and pension programs. The Veterans Administration became a cabinet level position under President George H. Bush, who declared that "There is only one place for veterans of America — in the cabinet room, at the table with the President of the United States of America."

Tools for Your Use

While these benefits are not new, they are not widely known either. The VA does not advertise their availability. Yet, as we age and need to preserve the resources we have saved during our working years and obtain the benefits we have earned, we must look for and expand the tools in our toolbox. (In this book I may often make references to "tools." One reason is that while I was in the Air Force, I was a carpenter/mason for three years. So I have a real appreciation for tools in all aspects of life.)

I didn't always have this appreciation, nor did the guys I worked with. When I enlisted, I was a 5′3″ female weighing only 97 pounds. Also, on my ASVAB, I incorrectly answered a question that had a picture of a screw driver and asked what kind it was. I said it was a Phillip's when it was actually a flathead screwdriver. Who would have thought the Air Force would have assigned such a small person with no experience to this kind of job? Not too many people and that's the reaction I got when I was stationed at my first duty station as well. My teammates would say, "What are we going to do with her? Put her in a corner and leave her by herself." But, after I got underfoot, especially while I was swinging a hammer all around them, they started paying attention and training me the right way to do my job. By reading this book, you will have the right tools and training you need to determine what benefits you could be eligible for, and the secret tips on how to get them.

Mission of the VA

Long before the VA created its mission statement, President Abraham Lincoln emphasized in his second Inaugural address on March 4, 1865, "the debt owed to America's veterans is to care for him who shall have borne the battle, and for his widow, and for his orphan."

That mission was later expanded "To serve America's veterans and their families as their principal advocate in ensuring that they receive the care, support and recognition they have __earned__ in service to this nation."

Earned is the key word. I hear from too many clients that they "don't want a handout" or "don't want to take away from other people who may need it more" or "don't want charity," and the list goes on. However, veterans' benefits are benefits that were earned due to the person's military service. That person sacrificed much, such as higher paying jobs, time with family, higher education, and many luxuries others take for granted in order to serve. When a person is elderly and in need of good health care, those benefits should not be ignored. Rejecting a benefit that has been earned is like leaving money on the table and walking away. Being denied those benefits by the VA is an injustice.

Difference in Treatment of "Compensation" vs. "Pension" Benefits

Former Veterans Administration Secretary Anthony Principi said that "America's veterans deserve the best health care and compensation we can provide."

In this book you will learn the difference between "Compensation" and "Pension." Note here, however, that Secretary Principi focuses on "compensation," which is specific to people who have been injured as a result of their military service.

Most senior citizens who served in the military; however,

are eligible for "pension" which is like a "distant cousin" to "compensation" benefits in the VA system. This knowledge can provide you with some insight as to the frustration that families feel as they try to obtain VA pension benefits for loved ones who are elderly, frail, and may pass away while waiting. It may feel as though the VA is deliberately not adjudicating the application so that the claimant will die and the VA will not have to pay anything. The truth is, the "pension" benefit is just not the VA's priority.

Hierarchy of the VA System

To completely appreciate the VA system, it is important to understand the VA hierarchy. The VA is the second largest federal government agency, which includes the following figure heads and departments:

A. Office of the Secretary of the VA is the highest position in the VA. The Secretary is appointed by the President of the United States.

B. Office of the General Counsel of the VA is also appointed by the President of the United States. The General Counsel serves as the Chief Legal Officer on all matter of law, litigation and legislation. The Office of the General Counsel (OGC) writes the laws that are submitted to Congress for approval. The OGC then interprets the laws, and when they don't like the successful advocacy that veterans receive from their lawyers, they change the laws. The purpose of the Office of General Counsel is to meet the legal needs of the VA, not the legal needs of the veterans. Its primary objective is to ensure the just and faithful execution of the laws, regulations and policies that the Secretary has responsibility for administering and by doing so, enable the department to accomplish its mission of service to our nation's veterans.

C. Veterans Benefits Administration (VBA)

The VBA provides an integrated program of veterans' benefits. The majority of benefits include the compensation benefit for service connected disabilities; pension benefits for war-time veterans who have non-service connected disabilities and meet certain financial criteria; burial benefits; rehabilitation assistance; home loans; and life insurance. Thus, the VBA has to do with "financial" monetary benefits.

D. Veterans Health Administration (VHA)

The VA has a nationwide system of VA medical centers and clinics, research centers, information research centers and domicilaries, which is akin to HUD housing for veterans.

E. National Cemetery System.

A discussion of the cemetery system will be discussed in Part V, Secrets 39-40.

At this point, imagine if you will, a soccer field. A soccer game consists of two different teams, is played according to a rule book, and has neutral officials ensuring that the game is played ethically. Now, picture the Veterans Administration as the soccer field, its employees as the diffcrent teams, and the Board of Veterans Appeals (hearing officers) as the officials. Further, consider that the teams are permitted to change or make up the rules as they go to best suit their needs, and the teammates can change teams anytime they want. Since the officials are tied to the field itself, they make rulings that are in the best interest of the field.

This is what it is like at the VA. The VA writes the laws, interprets the laws, and then changes the laws. The first-line hearing officers work for, and are paid by, the VA. The VA is the second largest federal agency. Its size alone may be its greatest weakness.

Laws, Rules, and Regulations Governing VA Benefits

The laws that govern all VA benefits are found in Title 38 of the United States Code. The United States Code is not extremely explanatory, rather, it bares just the nitty gritty, black and white law. In other words, the Code outlines a law but it doesn't really explain what it means. For an in-depth explanation of what the law means, we must turn to Title 38 of the Code of Federal Regulations (CFR). The CFR is where you need to eat, live, breathe and sleep if you want to know VA benefits inside and out.

VA adjudicators have their own adjudication manual to follow as well. The manual instructs the adjudicator on how to process a claim. To understand what is in the mind of the VA adjudicator, you must read the VA policy manual, the

M21-1 and the M21-1MR. The actual manual is the M21-1. But because the VA is always updating its manual, the updates are found in the M21-1MR. These manuals can be found on the internet at:

www.warms.vba.va.gov/m21_1.html and

www.warms.vba.va.gov/M21_1MR.html

In the manuals, you will find a table of contents. You will spend most of your time looking through parts four and five because that is where information about pension and death indemnity compensation (DIC) are found, especially pension information.

The Office of General Counsel also publishes its own opinions. These are like case law but without a judge. Attorneys and veterans send in questions, called "issues," to the General Counsel. These are new issues that have never been ruled on. The Office of General Counsel publishes its opinion, which has presidential effect on all future adjudications and appeals involving veterans' benefits under the laws that are administered by the VA. Thus, the General Counsel's interpretation on legal matters contained in such opinions is conclusive as to all VA officials and employees not only in the matter at hand, but also in future adjudications and appeals.

In the absence of a changing and controlling statute of regulation or case law, these opinions stand. One interesting aspect about General Counsel opinions is that not all of them are published (provided to the public). Therefore, neither practitioners nor veterans have access to all of the opinions. Nevertheless, the VA relies upon all the opinions they have previously issued when making a ruling. This can be problematic as practitioners and veterans have no way of knowing what exactly the VA is relying on when a decision is made.

Part II – Secret Money for Se:___

Most veterans are at least a little familiar with the VA health care system. Accessing the VA health care system can save the veteran a lot of money, but it doesn't **make** the veteran any money. We'll talk about the VA health care system later, in Part IV, but now I would like to share with you the secret money that most veterans know nothing about.

SECRET # 1

Senior citizen veterans or their surviving dependents can receive up to $1,949 per month ($23,396 per year) in tax free income. (This dollar amount is accurate through 2010, but usually increases each year on December 1st based on the federal cost of living adjustment increase.)

Veterans believe that they must be injured while on active duty to receive any monetary benefits from the VA. This is not correct.

Certain elderly veterans who have non-service connected

disabilities can receive a benefit called "Improved Pension." There are older versions of the program that have slightly different rules, but anyone who is applying for the benefits today would be applying for the Improved Pension. Improved Pension is a base level income which has two additional supplemental income levels depending on the person's level of health care need. The two supplemental levels are called Housebound Benefits and Aid and Attendance Benefits.

I'd like to share two stories about two clients of mine who benefited from receiving the Improved Pension with Aid and Attendance.

Robert is 82 years of age and has Alzheimer's disease. He and his wife, Suzanne, have been married for 62 years. Suzanne is fairly healthy but she falls a lot and is at risk of breaking her hip. Robert and Suzanne have one child, Jill, who has promised to keep Robert and Suzanne together as long as possible. Because home health care for both parents could easily exceed $12,000 per month, and because Jill believed her parents would benefit from socializing with others, she decided to move them into an assisted living facility. The cost of the assisted living facility for both is $5,300 per month. However, their combined monthly income is only $3,600. This means that Robert and Suzanne will have to pull approximately $1,700 each month from their retirement savings just to pay for the assisted living facility. This is in addition to their other continuing expenses, including medications, utilities, etc. Since Robert and Suzanne only have $120,000 in savings, they would easily spend through this money in less than six years; even faster if one of them had a medical crisis that required a higher level of care. Since both Robert and Suzanne are physically healthy and had parents who lived into their late 90's, running out of money is a serious concern for them. If Robert and Suzanne depleted all of their assets, they would be forced to move to a nursing home and apply for Medicaid. At that point, they may have to separate, live in different places, and lose their quality of life.

Because Robert served in the Army during World War II, he is considered a war-time veteran. War-time veterans who meet certain criteria that will be detailed later, may be eligible for income from the VA to assist with the cost of their health care. In this case, we were able to help Robert obtain $1,949 per month to help pay for his assisted living facility costs. This additional income has allowed Robert and Suzanne to continue living together in an environment that maintains their quality of life and dignity.

Mary was another client who was the widow of a Korean war-time veteran. Her husband had died several years ago and Mary never checked with the VA to see if there were any benefits she could receive. Mary had a stroke which affected her walking gait, speech, and memory. She has been living in an assisted living facility for four years. During that time, Mary's house, located in a retirement community out of state, was listed for sale without any interested buyers. Mary's only child, Charles, lost his job as a consultant and had his own child in college. Keep in mind, the economy began to deteriorate beginning in 2008 and by 2010 the housing and job markets were extremely depressed. Charles scheduled an appointment with me to discuss moving his mother to a nursing home and applying for Medicaid. He had run out of his own personal money and could no longer supplement the cost of his mother's care. Mary's house that was for sale had a line of credit that had to be paid off monthly or she would lose all of her equity through a fore-closure. The family was desperate. When I discussed nursing home care with Charles, he started to cry because he did not want his mother to live in a nursing home when the assisted living facility could provide all the care she needed — *if only they could afford it.*

I asked Charles if his mother were a veteran or a veteran's widow. He said, "yeah, but my dad never received any benefits and she won't either." I asked if he had heard about the improved pension with aid and attendance. Not surprisingly, he said that he had not. I asked him if an additional $1,056 per month would help to keep his mother at the assisted living facility so that she didn't have to live in a nursing home. He sat up in his chair and was very quiet; he wrote down some calculations without speaking; then suddenly overjoyed, he jumped out of his chair, rushed over to me and gave me a hug. Growing calmer, he told me that $795 was all they needed each month to bridge the shortfall in her income versus the assisted living facility costs.

At the end of our discussion, Charles' wife, Betty, asked me two very pointed questions: (1) "Could Mary have been receiving this money from the VA the entire time she lived in the assisted living facility?" I said, "yes." And then, she asked (2), "Why didn't anyone tell us about this?" and began to cry. The only explanation I could give was, "The VA is not advertising it and the community doesn't know about it."

At that point, I decided I would begin teaching my community, then the elder care attorney community, and now you, about these important benefits. So, what is this pension and how can you get it?

This is the one type of benefit that most veterans know nothing about and lawyers are just now learning about in order to help their elderly clients. VA pension is one of the best benefits veterans and their families can obtain because it is actual, real money in their pockets to help pay for home health care, assisted living facility costs, and nursing home care.

Most people want to live at home, or alternatively with their children. Or, if necessary, an assisted living facility, but the majority of my clients say they **do not want** to go to a nursing home. VA pension benefits can help veterans and their spouses live in higher, more independent levels of care arrangements longer.

What are the eligibility requirements? How do you qualify?

First of all, before we get to qualification details, you need to know that there are three different levels of pension. From our friends and fellow veterans, we always hear about "aid and attendance" as the benefit we should seek. However, "aid and attendance" is the third level out of three different levels of Improved Pension. Those levels are: (1) Low Income Pension; (2) Pension with Housebound; and (3) Pension with Aid and Attendance. The service record eligibility criteria are the same for each level. However, the medical and financial criteria are different at each level.

For the basic service record eligibility, the veteran must meet the following criteria (if the veteran is deceased, the widow applying for benefits must meet the same criteria based on the veteran's military service record):

A. The veteran must have served at least 90 days of active duty.

B. At least one day out of the 90 active duty days MUST have been during a war-time period.

The wartime periods as designated by Congress are as follows:

World War II: Dec. 7, 1941-Dec. 31, 1946

Korean War: June 27, 1950-Jan. 31, 1955

Vietnam Conflict: Aug. 5, 1964-May 7, 1975

(Feb. 28, 1961-May 7, 1975 if in the country of Vietnam)

Gulf War: August 2, 1990 through a

                            future date yet to be set by law

                            by Presidential Proclamation

For an example of war-time period and meeting the criteria, let's take a look at World War II. If the person went into the military on December 30, 1946, and served a total of 90 days, that would meet the requirements because at least one of those days was within that term, even though the war ended the very next day as set out by Congress.

Serving "during a war-time period" does not mean the veteran had to be in the actual war zone or combat theater. I served in the military during the Gulf War (Desert Storm). My unit was deployed to Turkey, which wasn't technically considered the war zone even though Scud missiles were flying overhead. Also, I could not deploy to Turkey because my commander believed that only men should go to war. So I remained at my base at Ramstein, Germany, providing support services. Nevertheless, my service still qualifies for war-time service because I was in the military during that time period. I didn't have to be on the front lines.

Additional criteria are:

C. The veteran must have received a discharge other than dishonorable.

D. The claimant and the household must have limited income and assets.

E. The claimant must have a permanent and total disability at the time of application.

There is one exception to item "e." Widows of veterans who are applying for benefits do not have to be disabled to qualify for the Low Income Pension only. However, if a veteran is only applying for Low Income Pension, he must be disabled. The disability does NOT have to be related to military service or the war-time period.

F. The disability the veteran has must be caused without willful misconduct of the veteran or due to the abuse of alcohol or drugs.

SECRET # 2

You can Qualify for a VA Pension Even if Your Income Exceeds the Limits

The VA will pay up to a maximum amount per month/year in pension, housebound, and aid and attendance. For example, the maximum for each level for the year 2010 is:

a. **Low Income Pension**

    i.   Veteran with no dependents

           $985month/$11,830year

    ii. Veteran with dependent spouse

           $1,291month/$15,493year

    iii.Widow of veteran

           $661month/$7,933year

b. **Pension with Housebound**

    i.   Veteran with no dependents

           $1,204month/$14,457year

    ii. Veteran with dependent spouse

           $1,510month/$18,120year

    iii.Widow of veteran

           $808month/$9,696year

c. Pension with Aid and Attendance

    i. Veteran with no dependents

$1,644month/$19,736year

   ii. Veteran with dependent spouse

$1,949month/$23,396year

 iii.Widow of veteran

$1,056month/$12,681year

 iv. Healthy Veteran with ill spouse

$1,291month/$15,493

Correspondingly, the maximum amount of income a veteran and the household can make from all other sources (i.e. Social Security, retirement pension, annuities, rents, interest on investments, etc.) is the same as the maximum amount the VA will pay out. For example, a veteran who is single with no dependents wants to apply for the low income pension. The income he receives from all other sources cannot exceed $985 per month. Likewise, for a veteran who is married and wants to apply for pension with aid and attendance, he and his wife jointly cannot make more than $1,949 in monthly income from any other source.

The black letter of the law says that if the veteran makes more than $985 or if the couple makes more than $1,949 in the above examples, then they will not be eligible for the VA pension benefits. If the veteran or the couple make less than the prescribed amount above, then VA will pay them an amount certain to bring their income up to $985 or $1,949, whichever example applies.

Thus, if the claimant has no income, the VA will pay up to the maximum amount of benefit based on the level of pension benefits being sought (assuming all other medical and service requirements are met). For example, if the veteran receives $600 per month in income from other sources, then the VA will pay the veteran $385 to bring his income up to the VA maximum income for low income pension.

Where the SECRET comes in is this — when you call the VA and inquire about applying for Improved Pension at any of the three levels, you will be asked the amount of your household income. If your answer indicates that the income is above the maximum limit the VA will pay, then the VA will advise you that you are not eligible for any benefits. With that answer, most families become discouraged and never apply for the benefit. Many people have incomes that exceed the permissible limit and feel they could never qualify.

However, what the VA does not tell you is that there are certain permissible deductions that are subtracted from your income BEFORE your income is compared to the maximum limits.

According to the regulations, the VA is required to take the gross income of the claimant and other household members, and subtract from that all recurring, non-reimbursed medical expenses. Only after having done this, the VA can then determine whether your income is above or below the permissible limits.

SECRET # 3

Recurring, non-reimbursed medical expenses of BOTH the veteran and the spouse are deductible from gross income.

Recurring, un-reimbursed medical expenses are costs paid out of pocket for medical expenses. These expenses typically include medical premiums, such as Medicare premiums, supplemental health care premiums, prescriptions, doctors' visits, travel to and from doctors' visits, home health care, assisted living facility care and nursing home care.

For example, let's say your gross income is $5,000 a month. You subtract out your Medicare premium ($96.40 for each spouse = $192.80), your supplemental health insurance premium ($125 for each spouse — $250), your medications ($500 for husband and $300 for wife = $800), and the home health care or assisted living facility costs ($4,200). Total recurring, un-reimbursed medical expenses in this example come to $5,442.80. Thus, recurring, un-reimbursed medical expenses exceed total income.

The goal we are trying to achieve, if we want to receive the maximum pension allowance from the VA, is that we zero out our income. If we do that, then the VA will pay the maximum amount permissible under the level of pension we qualify for medically. If the income is not zeroed out, that does not mean you are not eligible. It only means that the VA is not going to pay you the maximum. Instead, the VA will pay the difference between your excess income (after all permissible deductions) and the maximum permissible pension limit.

In the example above, the total recurring, non-reimbursed medical expenses exceeded the gross monthly income by $442.80. Thus, the VA should pay the claimant the maximum for any of the levels he or she is seeking. Assuming the veteran applied for pension with aid and attendance, the VA should pay $1,949 per month because in the example the veteran is married.

However, let's change the example slightly. Let's say the income is the same at $5,000 per month. All expenses stay the same except medications. The veteran receives his medications free from the VA instead of paying out of pocket, and his wife does not take any medications. Now their total recurring, non-reimbursed medical expenses are only $4,642.80 per month, an amount less than their combined monthly income. But this does not mean they are not eligible. Rather, the VA should pay the veteran approximately $1,591 ($5,000 income minus $4,642 = $358 excess income: $1,949 maximum pension minus $358 excess income = $1,591 payment by VA for pension with aid and attendance). This is a simplified version of the calculation the VA conducts. There is actually more that goes into the calculation that is beyond the scope of this book. Thus, the figures above may not be exactly the amount the VA would pay, but they are very close.

SECRET # 4

Family Members Can Be Paid Caregivers, which is a Deductible Expense

People usually begin to receive care in the home before they move to alternative living arrangements. A home health care provider can be a company that is certified, insured and bonded. Or, the care provider can be a non-family member, who may or may not be certified. Or, the caregiver can be a family member.

When people begin receiving in-home care, it is usually a family member providing that care. Typically, it begins with a daily phone call, then weekly or daily visits. The visits start to include bringing in meals, checking the mail, picking up the house, and paying bills. Sometimes family members move in with their loved one, or the elderly person moves in with the family member. There are many reasons why this is the most common course. Elderly persons do not always acknowledge that they need additional help. Also, they enjoy having their children or other family members visiting more often. Hiring a stranger can be a frightening prospect due to the high risk of financial exploitation or abuse and neglect. Moreover, hiring a reputable elder care company that is insured and bonded can be expensive. So, families try to honor the desires of their loved ones by keeping them at home, while at the same time trying to stretch their assets as far as possible. Hence, the family caregiver.

Should the Family Caregiver be Paid?

There can be a huge debate among families as to whether a family member should be paid to take care of another family member, or if they should just do it out of love and affection. I am of the mind set that a family member SHOULD be paid in most circumstances to take care of a loved one. Let me illustrate with a story.

Karen's father, Ken, is very physically healthy and is adamant that he wants to live at home. Yet, he has moderate short-term memory loss that makes it unsafe to leave him unsupervised for periods exceeding two-hour blocks. Karen spent two years "checking in" on her father, arranging doctors' appointments, accompanying Ken to the doctor, performing light housekeeping chores, and paying his bills. These arrangements take several hours per week, forcing Karen to reduce her formal work hours with her employer. Ultimately Karen quit her job and moved in with her father. Now she has no income to pay her own bills, which include a cell phone, car insurance, mortgage and maintenance on her own house, etc. Some people, including Karen's brother, might say, "But she is living with her father rent free and he pays all the food and utilities." Sure. But if you put a dollar value on Karen's time, services and loss of employment benefits, it would far exceed that which she receives in "free rent."

Additionally, Karen no longer receives health care benefits through her work and now must pay privately for her own policy, an expensive proposition. Her Social Security benefits payable at age 65 will be reduced due to a gap in work history. There are a lot of silent, yet severe, consequences when a person quits working to become a caregiver for a family member. These are the reasons they should receive adequate compensation. If they were not available or willing, a hired caregiver through a reputable company would cost no less than $12-$21 per hour, much more than what a family caregiver would usually charge or accept for the same service.

For veterans' benefits purposes, the money paid to a family caregiver, as long as it is not the veteran's spouse, can be a deductible medical expense. Therefore, if a family member is providing the services anyway, and paying them can assist in obtaining money from the VA, then it is a good decision to pay the family member.

Three Cautionary Notes:

1. The family caregiver must report the caregiving income received to the Internal Revenue Service (IRS) just as they would any other income received.

The income received may place the caregiver in a higher tax bracket, causing them to owe more taxes. Before incurring additional income and possible tax consequences, speak with a tax professional (certified public accountant) and an attorney who is accredited by the VA.

2. In certain circumstances, you may NOT be able to

deduct the family caregiver costs as a deductible expense.

As mentioned earlier, there are three different levels of Improved Pension — low income pension, pension with housebound, and pension with aid and attendance. A complete description of each follows.

But for now, it is imperative for you to understand that if the person who needs the caregiver (the veteran or the widowed spouse) is rated by the VA as needing only the housebound level of care, then the family member caregiver MUST be certified as a licensed medical provider OR be under the direct supervision of a medical provider.

Oddly enough, when the claimant's level of care increases to the most severe level and he qualifies for the pension with aid and attendance level of care from another person, the family caregiver no longer needs to be a medically licensed provider. Instead, at this level the family caregiver can be any family member except a spouse.

To summarize — paying a family caregiver to provide services can be a deductible medical expense. However, if the VA rates the claimant as in need of "housebound benefits," then the family caregiver must be a certified medical provider (i.e. nurse, etc.). However, if the claimant is rated in need of "aid and attendance," then the family caregiver needs no certifications at all for the expense to be deductible.

3. Family Caregiver should be paid at the local Fair Market Value

There are different levels of home health care. The most basic level is called companion care or custodial care. Individuals providing companion care are usually providing supervisory care only to ensure the person is safe in the surrounding environment. The caregiver does not need to have any certifications. This level caregiver is generally paid $8-$12 per hour.

The next level of caregiver is a certified nurse's aide (CNA). Before I joined the Air Force, I was a CNA and worked in both a nursing home and a home health care company providing companion care. Before becoming a CNA, I had to take a written test as well as an on-the-job test that included taking a person's temperature, blood pressure, etc. CNAs are generally paid $10-$14 per hour.

The next level is either a licensed practical nurse (LPN) or licensed vocational nurse (LVN). These practitioners are usually found primarily in nursing homes and not in home health care settings. The last level is that of registered nurse (RN). Registered nurses will assist in home health care situations where there is a higher level of care need. Examples might include wound dressings, insulin shots, bed sores, etc. Nurses at this level generally make from \$16-\$28 per hour.

The family caregiver should research fair market value rates for the level of qualification she matches to determine what rate to charge. Family caregivers can certainly give a discount to their family member, but should never charge more than the local market rate.

SECRET # 5

The Entire Cost for an Assisted Living Facility is a Deductible Expense

With regard to assisted living facility charges, the VA is supposed to deduct the entire amount of the cost without needing to break out rental costs, medical costs, food costs, etc.

To assist in ensuring the VA makes the proper deduction, you should get a letter from the assisted living facility that details when the veteran (or widowed spouse) mov

total monthly charge. The letter should also have a statement similar to the following: "We provide the following services: medication assistance or administration, supervision, transportation to doctors' appointments, light housekeeping, etc." You would not want to submit the actual billing statement from the assisted living facility because it may itemize each cost and call the room-and-board expenses "rent." If you provide the VA with a bill that is itemized, they will try to not include all of the expenses and argue that they are not "medical" expenses. That is why it is better to get the letter from the facility instead.

Nevertheless, if the VA does deny a portion of the assisted living facility cost for any reason, then you should get a physician's order that prescribes this level of care. The physician's prescription should also make clear that the claimant needs to live in this type of controlled environment because he requires protection from the potential daily hazards of his environment. Therefore, all services provided by the assisted living facility are necessary for the required level of care and; thereby, considered a medical expense for VA purposes. If the spouse lives in an assisted living facility as well (either the same one or a different one), those expenses are deductible as well.

I had a client come see me because he was denied the full benefits due him. The VA did not include his wife's medical expenses as a deduction from their income. Both the veteran and his wife lived in an assisted living facility and the VA did not deduct the wife's portion of the expenses. The VA laws in the Code of Federal Regulations (CFR) clearly explain that the VA is to deduct the spouse's medical expenses as well. In this case, my remedy was to write a letter called a "Notice of Disagreement" and send it to the VA with copies of the CFR. The VA re-adjudicated the claim and awarded the benefits.

SECRET # 6

You can Qualify for VA Pension Even if Your Assets Exceed the Limit

To receive the VA pension, your assets (net worth) must be under a certain dollar amount. However, there is no particular dollar amount specified by the VA as to what is over and what is under the limit. The standard (and I say that loosely) is whether you have "sufficient means" to pay for your own care. How is that for a nice bright-line standard?

Who determines whether you have sufficient means? The individual VA adjudicator assigned to your file.

Does the VA adjudicator have personal discretion as to how he or she defines "sufficient means?" You bet! The M21-1 and M21-1MR adjudicator's manual explains that the adjudicator has extreme discretion. Nevertheless, the manual does outline suggested guidelines for the adjudicator when calculating "sufficient means." A number of variables must be taken into consideration when making a net worth determination. The factors are:

– Income from other sources

– Family expenses (non-medical expenses which the adjudicator can consider, but does not have to consider — and most often does not consider)

– The claimant's age/life expectancy (thus, if two people have the same level of net worth, but one is 10 years older than the other, the younger one may be approved for benefits while the older one may be denied due to excessive net worth)

A commonly used measure of acceptable net worth, and an amount which can be found in the M21-1 as a guideline for adjudicators is $80,000 or less in assets. The amount is the same whether the claimant is married or single. The reason there is no distinction in asset limits whether the claimant is married or single is that there is only one claimant. The claimant is either the veteran or it is the surviving spouse of the veteran. When the veteran is alive, the veteran is always the claimant. If the veteran is dead, the surviving spouse is the claimant. Thus, there is always only one claimant and the asset limit for the claimant, as a guide, is $80,000 or less.

In the past, the guideline figure was $50,000. Many lawyers and veteran service organizations still advise people to keep their assets under the old $50,000 limit. Some lawyers erroneously tell people that if you are married it is $80,000 and if you are single it is $50,000. As discussed previously, none of that makes any difference. What does make a difference is that if your assets are above $80,000 you will definitely be denied. If your assets are below $80,000, you may or may not be approved depending on the other factors considered, such as your age. For example, an attorney friend of mine told me about a married client of his who only had $30,000 in assets, very high medical expenses compared to their income, and was still denied VA pension benefits. The reasoning the VA adjudicator used was the veteran's age. However, even when doing the age analysis, the veteran was sure to run out of money well before his life expectancy expired. See below for an explanation of how the VA calculates an award based on age.

Age Analysis Calculation

Because the VA has begun to emphasize a claimant's age when determining excessive net worth, let's take a closer look at the age analysis process. The VA began instructing its caseworkers to perform an age analysis to determine financial need. Only people who have a financial need for the pension are awarded the pension. It is presumed that the older you are, the fewer assets you need to take care of yourself. So a person who is 98 years old who has $70,000 may be determined ineligible for pension benefits while a 78-year-old veteran with $70,000 might be deemed eligible simply because of his age.

The complicated calculation goes like this:

The VA calculates your life expectancy based on your age and compares it to the chart in the M21-1MR, Part V, Subpart iii, Chapter 1, Section J; there is no difference whether the person is male or female (i.e. 80 years old is 7.9 year life expectancy for both men and women, according to the VA life expectancy tables).

Next, the VA takes the value of your annual income and multiplies that by your life expectancy (i.e. $40,000 annual income times 7.9 years = $316,000)

Then, the VA adds the above $316,000 to your asset level of $75,000, which totals $391,000.

Lastly, the VA calculates your deductible recurring, non-reimbursed medical expenses that are projected over your life expectancy (i.e. annual deductible medical expenses are $71,000 multiplied by 7.9 life expectancy = $560,900).

In the example above, the veteran's net worth of $391,000 is not sufficient to pay for the veteran's needs over the veteran's life expectancy of 7.9 years, and thus, the veteran should be awarded pension income by the VA. If, however, the projected deductible medical expenses had been less than

$391,000 for the duration of the life expectancy of the veteran, then the veteran should be denied pension benefits.

According to the VA formula, if your assets are greater than your expenses for that same life expectancy time span, then you should be denied.

SECRET # 7

Trained attorneys who know VA laws and who are accredited by the VA can assist you in preserving your excess resources while still being awarded the pension.

For example, knowing the difference between what the VA counts as part of your net worth and what the VA excludes can make a big difference. One of my clients, Sarah, had a bank account with $120,000 in it. Sarah assumed she was not eligible for any benefits. However, she did not know one important fact — the VA is supposed to reduce her net worth by subtracting out the value of assets that are co-owned by another person who does not live with her. Since Sarah's daughter, Jodi, and her son, Jason, were both co-owners on the bank account, Sarah's portion was only one-third of $120,000, or $40,000. This is well below the $80,000 guideline and assuming Sarah's age analysis does not bar her eligibility, she should be awarded the pension.

There are many other laws like the ones above that the VA is not going to tell a claimant about. And the laws change regularly. Therefore, if you think you might be eligible for VA benefits, or COULD be eligible for benefits, it is incumbent upon you to seek out a competent elder care attorney who is accredited by the VA. The attorney will have YOUR best interest in mind when devising a specific plan based on your situation. Everyone's asset situation, health care situation, and family circumstances are different. The above is just one "tool" in the toolbox that competent attorneys are familiar with when creating an asset preservation plan for you. Preserving the assets you have while also obtaining the VA benefit will provide you the flexibility to live the quality of life you deserve while also getting the level of care you need.

Medical Qualification for Improved Pension

Now that you understand how to qualify for the VA pension financially — by meeting the income and asset requirements — it is important for you to understand how to qualify medically. Each level of Improved Pension requires different levels of medical need.

Low Income Pension

Low income pension is the basic level of Improved Pension. This benefit is the equivalent of Social Security's Supplemental Security Income (SSI). Veterans who are under the age of 65, disabled to the extent that they are unemployable, cannot maintain gainful employment, and it is not expected that their condition will improve, may receive low income pension from the VA. The veteran must prove his or her disability. If the veteran has been deemed disabled by Social Security, this determination can be used as presumptive evidence to the VA. The VA may, however, require the veteran to have a medical examination by a VA physician.

SECRET # 8

If the veteran is 65 years old or older, the VA presumes disability, and it does not have to be proven.

SECRET # 9

If the veteran is deceased and the surviving spouse is applying for low income pension, the spouse can be of ANY age and does NOT have to be disabled.

Pension with Housebound Benefits

Housebound benefits are available to a veteran or widow of a veteran who is determined to be disabled and is essentially confined to the home. Among other things, that means the claimant is not driving anymore. There is one exception to the "no driving" rule — the claimant may drive to doctors' appointments, the pharmacy, and grocery store to buy necessities *IF no other means of transportation is available.* Otherwise, the claimant shouldn't be driving or the claim for benefits is likely to be denied.

"Disability" within the housebound context is proven in one of two ways:

1. Having a single, permanent disability rated as 100% disabling under the VA disability rating schedule, and essentially confined to the home.

(I'm not talking about a service-connected disability, but you have to have a disability that would be considered 100% if it were measured under the VA schedule.)

OR

2. You have two different disabilities and one is rated 100% disabling and the other is rated at 60% disabling, but in this case you do not have to be confined to the home.

So the claimant who has two different disabilities, one rated at 100% and the other rated at least at 60%, can still be driving a car. In that case, the claimant's actions would not be limited by the VA because the claimant does not have to be confined to the home.

Again, as with low income pension, if a person is seeking pension with housebound benefits, no disability rating is required for people who are 65 years of age or older because the VA assumes they are disabled. However, even if you are 65 years of age or above and you do not have to prove disability, you do, in fact, still have to prove you are housebound, i.e., the additional element that you're confined to the home. Failure to prove this higher level of care need will result in a denial of benefits.

How do you prove that you are housebound?

Obtain a physician's affidavit or statement that details your daily activities and limitations. The doctor's affidavit should state that you are not driving around town, that you are getting meals-on-wheels, and/or other such assistance that homebound seniors frequently obtain.

As a reminder, for pension with housebound benefits, a veteran with no dependents can receive up to $1,204 per month in tax free income from the VA. A veteran with one dependent (usually a spouse) can receive up to $1,510 per month, and a housebound widow without dependents can receive up to $808 per month. These are the 2010 figures. When these amounts change, the change date is December 1st of each year.

SECRET # 10

Pension with Aid and Attendance is Easier to Obtain than Housebound Benefits

Pension with aid and attendance is the highest level of Improved Pension income the VA will pay. Likewise, the VA requires a claimant to have the most severe care needs at this level. However, I find that it is actually easier for my clients to obtain pension with aid and attendance than it is to obtain pension with housebound benefits. Since aid and attendance benefits pay more, we always apply for this level of need first.

Aid and attendance benefits are available to a veteran or widow of a veteran who meets the following medical conditions:

1. The claimant is blind. If the claimant is blind, he or she would automatically qualify for this level of care and payment by the VA (assuming all other military and financial requirements are met).

OR

2. The claimant is living in a skilled nursing home (not to be confused with an assisted living facility or a personal care home).

OR

3. The claimant is unable to dress, undress, keep himself clean and presentable, needs assistance with using the restroom or is incontinent, or has a physical or mental incapacity that requires assistance on a regular basis to protect himself from daily environmental hazards.

Most of my clients fall into the third category above — needing the assistance of another with the activities of daily living or custodial supervision due to mental incapacity and memory loss.

For example, I had a client, Alice, with progressive Alzheimer's disease. She could bathe herself with cuing (reminders). Alice could go to the restroom and dress herself without any assistance. She could also eat with cuing; however, she wouldn't eat unless someone told her to do so. Alice definitely needed assistance with her medication administration. But, Alice was still very physically healthy, and relatively young (74) as compared to many of my clients. She could engage in conversation, but she wouldn't remember it minutes later.

A neighbor noticed that Alice was leaving her front door

open at all hours, would not turn off the stove, and had flooded the apartment below hers after forgetting to turn off the bathtub faucet. Obviously, Alice was not safe in her own environment. Even though she could do many things for herself, her inability to protect herself and her need for supervised assistance made her eligible for pension with aid and attendance.

Again, to summarize the financial benefit of obtaining pension with aid and attendance, a veteran with no dependents can receive up to $1,644 per month. A veteran with a dependent, which is typically a spouse, can receive up to $1,949 a month, a total of $23,396 a year. And a widow with no dependents can receive up to $1,056 per month, which is just over $12,000 a year.

When I have asked clients, "Would an extra $23,000 a year benefit you?" not a single one has ever said, "no, I don't need that." It can really help, especially if the goal is to stay at home or in an assisted living facility without prematurely needing to move to a nursing home strictly because resources ran out.

SECRET # 11

A veteran who is healthy but has a spouse who is disabled, CAN receive Improved Pension — Low Income Pension

We have been discussing veterans who are disabled and widows of veterans who are disabled applying for VA pension. There is another category wherein the pension is payable. It is in the case of a healthy, living veteran who has a spouse with disabilities.

The situation is this: Sam is 79 and lives at home. He still drives, takes his vitamins, and golfs three times a week. Sam is the primary caregiver for his wife, Imogene. However, that role is becoming increasingly difficult for Sam because Imogene continues to have small strokes that affect her mobility. Imogene is overweight and a fall risk. Therefore, Sam is exploring alternative living arrangements. He would like to move Imogene to an assisted living facility but is afraid he cannot afford it. When Sam was looking at possible assisted living facilities for Imogene, he heard about some VA "aid and attendance" benefit. When he called the veteran's representative, he was told he could not get anything from the VA because he was still alive and healthy. Fortunately Sam did not give up on his quest. Had he given up, he would have lost the opportunity to obtain $1,291 per month, or $15,493 per year.

Instead, Sam was told by his friend to come and see me. During our consultation, I explained to Sam that because he is over the age of 65 (and presumed to be disabled), and because he and his wife's gross monthly income is depleted after deducting recurring, non-reimbursed medical expenses (or would be if she moved into an assisted living facility), and they have limited resources otherwise, Sam could apply for and receive Low Income Pension.

It is true that Sam will not be able to obtain pension with housebound nor aid and attendance because Sam is healthy and not housebound or in need of another person to help him with his activities of daily living. Nevertheless, Sam is the VA claimant, Sam is 65 years of age or older, and Sam has limited income and assets that are even more limiting when deducting his and his wife's deductible medical expenses.

Having this one piece of knowledge, a secret that is not widely publicized, opened the door to so many more options for Sam and Imogene. Now Sam can sleep peacefully knowing that his wife is getting the level of care she needs, and that he will not have to jeopardize his health or quality of life.

Money for Service Connected Disabilities

Public support is greater for compensation benefits for veterans injured during combat or while on active duty than it is for other VA benefits. Society at large is of the opinion that it is only right that veterans who participate in the country's wars and are wounded as a result are due monetary compensation from that society. Consequently, the VA as an institution protects the compensation program before all other benefits programs.

What defines a veteran with a service connected disability?

A veteran with a service connected disability is one who suffered an injury or disease while on active duty and the injury/disease was the result of his or her service or was exacerbated by that service. That person may be entitled to a monthly income called compensation.

Veterans are entitled to disability compensation if they

meet the following criteria:

  – They were discharged or released under conditions other than dishonorable.

  – The disease or injury was incurred or aggravated in the line of duty.

SECRET # 12

You do not have to have been injured while working.

Most of us think "in the line of duty" means that you were working when you were injured. When you are in the military, you are on call 24/7. Consequently, if you are in the military and you are injured, whether you are working or not, it is considered to be in the line of duty.

For example, when I was stationed in Germany, I went on a ski trip where I fell and hurt myself. I was flat on my back and my neck popped. I was afraid to move. Nevertheless, I could not lie there forever. So, I wiggled my hands and feet and then got up. I was sore for a few days, but no permanent damage. However, if I had been significantly hurt and it lasted longer than just that moment, that disability, that injury, would have been considered to have been sustained in the line of duty because I was in the military when it happened, even though it wasn't while I was working.

If you think you have to have been working when you sustained an injury, you are not alone. Most veterans think that you had to have been engaged in doing your work to get your benefits. However, that is just not the case.

Here are the rules:

– You had to have been on active duty to be considered "in the military." To determine whether a person was on "active duty," you will need to look at the veteran's discharge papers.

– The disease or injury, incurred or aggravated, while in the line of duty and cannot be as a result of the veteran's own willful misconduct or abuse of alcohol or drugs.

Here's an example. Let's say I am in the shower on a Saturday, a non-working day. I am on active duty in the military. I slip and fall; I hit my head on the tub and now I have severe migraines that prevent me from working a full day, and so I am disabled. This is a qualifying injury for a VA service connected disability.

Now, let's take that scenario one step further. I was out the night before, and I was drinking all night and got totally intoxicated. I get up in the morning still intoxicated. I climb into the shower, slip and fall and hit my head, and now I have migraines because of it. The VA could argue that the injury was due to my own willful misconduct or abuse of alcohol or drugs and would deny my claim.

SECRET # 13

Entitlement to service connected compensation is not barred by the veteran's employment.

Service connected compensation is a system similar to worker's compensation in the civilian world. You are being paid for your loss of function or use of whatever part of your body has been injured. When you become injured and you prove the elements outlined above (as well as some other requirements that we are going to talk about below), the VA will pay you a monthly income called compensation in an effort to make you whole for your loss, just as worker's compensation does.

Assigning a Disability Rating

The VA assigns a disability rating to the associated disability. The rating ranges from 0% to 100%. The ratings are increased in increments of 10. Thus, it goes from 0% to 10% to 20% to 30%, and so on all the way up to 100%, depending on the type and severity of the disability. The amount paid through compensation is based on the rating percentage that the VA has awarded you.

SECRET # 14

A 0% rating is still a benefit.

If you are rated as disabled but receive a 0% rating, you will not receive monetary compensation; however, simply having a service connected disability gives you priority in the VA health care system. It also gives you the ability to submit a request to increase your rating percentage if your disability becomes more severe over time. Since you are already in the VA system at that time, your adjudication of the increased rating should be quicker than the initial application process. So don't underestimate a 0% rating.

SECRET # 15

A 30% or higher service connected disability rating will pay you a higher amount of money if you have a spouse or dependents.

Once your disability rating reaches at least 30%, then you will be paid an additional stipend for having dependents. The disability rating of 30% or more can be a combination of several disabilities, all of which individually may be less than 30%. For example, if you are deemed 10% disabled for hearing loss, 10% disabled for hay-fever, and 20% disabled for a bad back, your combined disability rating may be 30% or more (the VA has a formulary to combine disability ratings, they do not just add them all up to get the rating).

SECRET # 16

A 70% or above rating will allow a claimant to reside in a federal VA nursing home, usually at no charge.

Having the option of using a federal VA nursing home, usually at no charge, can be a distinct benefit to an elderly veteran. Neither the income nor the assets of the veteran and the spouse are factors in qualifying. This option can save up to $120,000 or more per year for the veteran.

SECRET # 17

When rated at 100% disability or if rated as unemployable, you will receive the highest rating and the highest pay. Plus, if you are in need of the additional aid of another person to help with your activities of daily living (walking, bathing, dressing, toileting, etc.) there is an added supplement to your compensation called "aid and attendance."

This is a different benefit than the pension with aid and attendance benefit discussed above. Here's an example. One of my clients had suffered a traumatic brain injury while in the Air Force. Years later he developed severe memory loss and also lost the ability to make reasonable decisions. He was only 44 years old. Because of his injury, he was not able to work and he needed the supervision of another person to make sure he was safe in his environment. The brain damage he suffered affected his ability to make rational decisions. Often his wife would find him riding recklessly on his four-wheeler and placing his minor child in dangerous situations. He was awarded a 100% disability rating. Because of the need for supervision, it was also determined that he was in need of aid and attendance. His monthly benefit from the VA was over $4,000. He was also paid extra because he had a wife and a minor child.

SECRET # 18

Service connected disability income is not barred or reduced if you have other income (i.e. from working or from Social Security, etc.).

Since service connected disability compensation is based purely on loss due to a disability, and not on a person's income or net worth, receiving income from other sources is permissible. Moreover, you will not lose your benefits if you are still employed.

SECRET # 19

The level of your assets does not matter for service connected disability compensation.

Compensation is not based on how much money you have, the income you make or any other financial consideration. Thus, you do NOT have to spend down your assets to qualify for service connected disability compensation benefits.

SECRET # 20

VA compensation is tax free income.

Veterans are often concerned that if they apply for service connected disability compensation, that they will be taxed on the income and, thus, have to pay more income tax. This is not correct. Both VA compensation and VA pension are tax free income.

Elements of Proof for Service Connected Disability

In order to receive service connected disability compensation, the veteran must prove three essential elements.

(1) There must be a medical diagnosis of current disability;

(2) There must be medical or lay evidence of an in-service occurrence or the aggravation of a disease or injury; and

(3) There must be a nexus between the current disability and that in-service occurrence. So let me give you a personal example.

When I was in the military, I was a carpenter. I sustained an injury. Here is how it happened: I weighed 97 pounds when I enlisted. The guys I worked with were much larger than me. Because I worked in a traditional man's job, I was trying to prove myself as someone who they would want to work with, and would want to be on their team. We had a masonry job to complete. Masonry involves handling a lot of concrete and bags of plaster. Our job site was on the interior of a building, up some 34 stair steps.

I was getting my bag of plaster, which weighed 60

pounds, from the truck to take upstairs to do my job. My co-worker, superior in rank, was on the back of the truck handing me a bag of plaster. I threw it on my shoulder and turned around to walk about 40 yards, and then up 34 stairs. My co-worker, put his hand on my head to stop me from leaving. He threw another bag on my shoulder. That meant I was carrying 120 pounds and walking with both bags on my shoulders. I made it to the end of the long hallway. I climbed the stairs and made it almost all the way to the top. I was about four steps away from the top when my legs began to give way. Fortunately, a good friend of mine, Sgt. McVey, was at the top. All I could do was look at him and give him an expression like, "you'd better take these bags because I'm going down." He saved the bags and he saved me.

But in the process I developed a hemorrhoid. Carrying more than you are supposed to carry apparently puts strain on your innards. I sought treatment at the military medical facility on base. The treatment consisted of basically eating soft foods and using Preparation H. This event is documented in my medical records. I can show a specific incident.

Fast forward to years later. My enlistment ended and I left

military service. I don't know if you have experienced hemorrhoids or not, but I will just share with you that they come and go. They are always there but the discomfort comes and goes. Sometimes it feels like shards of glass are passing through. So the last thing you want is a doctor poking around all the time in your private areas. So I just kind of grinned and bore it when I had to and; otherwise, I was comfortable. Like many people, I wanted to avoid going to the doctor.

Seven years after leaving the military I founded my law firm. I knew that my emphasis was going to be on helping elderly veterans obtain the benefits they had earned. So, I thought, "what better education than going through the application process myself." I can do my own application. I can fill it out and see first-hand what my clients will be going through when they file claims.

At this time, my hemorrhoid was acting up. I still didn't want to go to the doctor. Nevertheless, I went to the VA regional office to file my application for a service connected disability. The VA representative asked if I had been to the doctor lately. I had not. He said, "well, you are going to have

to go because we need medical evidence of a current disability."
I chose not to go. Thus, I was denied benefits. The VA
acknowledged, in writing, that I incurred the injury while in
the military. They acknowledged that it was in my medical
records, but they denied me because I couldn't show that my
injury was currently disturbing me. All of the three essential
elements must be proven to the VA to receive benefits.

Four Step Adjudication Process

Once the VA receives a claim for service connected disability benefits, it processes the claim by following a four step
adjudication process.

(1) Upon receipt of the application at the VA regional
office in the state where you live, the VA will determine if the veteran meets the service discharge
requirements.

(2) The VA will determine if the three essential elements
have been met.

(3) If so, the VA will then determine the severity of
the disability and adjudicate a disability rating of
0%-100%.

(4) Then, the VA will establish the effective date for the disability, the onset date. Typically, you will get paid from the month after you filed the application. So even if you were disabled in 1980, if you don't file an application until 2007, the onset date will likely be from 2007 and forward.

SECRET # 21

Surviving Spouses and Dependents of Service Connected Disabled Veterans can file a claim for benefits too.

Veterans, while alive, file their own claims. When a veteran dies there are certain surviving family members — dependents — who can file claims on their own behalf. These are called "death" claims.

The extent to which survivors can apply for and obtain death claims are beyond the scope of this book for elderly veterans. However, there are a couple of secrets I want to share with you before moving on.

SECRET # 22

The veteran and the surviving spouse did NOT have to be married to each other while the veteran was in the military or when the veteran was injured.

A surviving spouse is a person who was married to the veteran for at least one year prior to the veteran's death, and who was not separated from the veteran at the time of death. I get a lot of questions about whether a divorced spouse can get benefits. The answer is NO because she is no longer a spouse. In this situation, we have an EX-spouse, not a widowed spouse or a surviving spouse.

SECRET # 23

If a veteran dies while his or her claim is pending before the VA (submitted but not yet approved), the surviving spouse can continue to pursue the veteran's claim for benefits (accrued benefits). In addition, the surviving spouse can make his or her own, independent claim for benefits (death indemnity claim).

If the veteran was receiving, or should have been receiving, compensation benefits at the time of his death, his spouse is eligible to receive compensation for the rest of her life. The spouse's compensation benefit may not be the same dollar amount the veteran was receiving, but it still may be worthwhile to pursue.

SECRET # 24

Veterans who served in the country of Vietnam anytime from February 28, 1961 through May 7, 1975, and later developed certain illnesses or diseases, are presumed to have been exposed to Agent Orange and, thus, have a service connected disability.

Veterans may be eligible for disability compensation and health care benefits for diseases that the VA has recognized as associated with exposure to Agent Orange and other herbicides:

Acute and Subacute Peripheral Neuropathy

A nervous system condition that causes numbness, tingling, and motor weakness. Under the VA's rating regulations, it must be at least 10% disabling within one year of exposure to Agent Orange and resolve within two years after the date it began.

AL Amyloidosis

A rare disease caused when an abnormal protein, amyloid, enters tissues or organs.

B Cell Leukemias

Cancers which affect B cells, such as hairy cell leukemia.

Chloracne (or Similar Acneform Disease)

A skin condition that occurs soon after dioxin exposure and looks like common forms of acne seen in teenagers. Under VA's rating regulations, chloracne (or other acneform disease similar to chloracne) must be at least 10% disabling within 1 year of exposure to Agent Orange.

Chronic Lymphocytic Leukemia

A disease that progresses slowly with increasing production of excessive numbers of white blood cells.

Diabetes Mellitus (Type 2)

A disease characterized by high blood sugar levels resulting from the body's inability to respond properly to the hormone insulin.

Hodgkin's Disease

A malignant lymphoma (cancer) characterized by progressive enlargement of the lymph nodes, liver, and spleen, and by progressive anemia.

Ischemic Heart Disease

A disease characterized by a reduced supply of blood to the heart.

Multiple Myeloma

A cancer of specific bone marrow cells that is characterized by bone marrow tumors in various bones of the body.

Non-Hodgkin's Lymphoma

A group of cancers that affect the lymph glands and other lymphatic tissue.

Parkinson's Disease

A motor system condition with symptoms that include trembling of the limbs and face and impaired balance.

Porphyria Cutanea Tarda

A disorder characterized by liver dysfunction and by thinning and blistering of the skin in sun-exposed areas. Under the VA's rating regulations, it must be at least 10% disabling within one year of exposure to Agent Orange.

<u>Prostate Cancer</u>

Cancer of the prostate; one of the most common cancers among men.

<u>Respiratory Cancers</u>

Cancers of the lung, larynx, trachea, and bronchus.

<u>Soft Tissue Sarcoma (other than Osteosarcoma, Chondrosarcoma, Kaposi's sarcoma, or Mesothelioma)</u>

A group of different types of cancers in body tissues such as muscle, fat, blood and lymph vessels, and connective tissues.

The list above is found on the VA's website at www.publichealth.va.gov/exposures/agentorange/diseases.asp#veterans.

SECRET # 25

You didn't have to serve in Vietnam to incur a presumptive illness.

There are five listings in Title 38 of the Code of Federal Register section 3.309, that list presumptive illnesses in the following categories: Chronic diseases, tropical diseases, disease specific to POWs, radiation exposed veterans or radiogenic, and exposure to herbicides (listed above). You can go to: www.warms.vba.va.gov/regs/38CFR/BOOKB/PART3/S3_309.DOC for a complete list of presumptive illnesses as approved by Congress.

SECRET # 26

Amyotrophic Lateral Sclerosis (ALS), also known as Lou Gherrig's Disease, may be a presumptive service connected disease.

If you were diagnosed with ALS while on active duty or within one year from your date of discharge, your disease may be presumed to be service connected. If you were not diagnosed while in service or within a year of discharge, but you can prove with medical evidence or otherwise that you now have ALS, and that you had symptoms of ALS within the one-year period following discharge, you may still be eligible for service connected benefits.

If you have a condition that is listed on the presumed

illnesses list, then you would only need to apply for VA compensation benefits without the additional necessity to provide information that would otherwise link your illness to your service.

I was giving a presentation on veterans' benefits to a group of lawyers. The speech was focused primarily on non-service connected benefits available to seniors. However, I did mention the presumptive listings for service connected conditions. After the presentation a lawyer approached me and said he was in Vietnam. To every man that I know who served in Vietnam, my first comment is: If you are ever diagnosed with prostate cancer (which many men are), FILE A CLAIM FOR BENEFITS. Because he was African-American (thus, at a higher risk), I also told him that if he is ever diagnosed with diabetes type II, to file a claim. He shared with me that he does have diabetes type II and that, just the week before, he was diagnosed with prostate cancer. He had no idea he could file a claim for VA service connected benefits, and that his illnesses were presumed to be due to his military service.

Part III – Application Process for Improved Pension Benefits (with Aid and Attendance)

We are going to move on now into the application processing system. Applications for service connected disability claims are filed with the VA Regional Office (VARO in the state where the veteran lives. Claims for Improved Pension are also generally filed at the VA Regional Office (VARO). However, an application for improved pension may alternatively be filed directly with the Pension Center (the place that adjudicates the claim). There are only three Pension Management Centers for the entire nation:

(1) ST. PAUL PENSION MANAGEMENT CENTER

Pension Management Center (335/21P)

PO BOX 11000

St. Paul, MN 55111-0000

Fax: 1-612-970-5724

(2) MILWAUKEE VA PENSION CENTER

PO BOX 342000

Milwaukee, WI 53234-9907

Fax: 414-902-9470

Phone: 877-294-6380

(3) PHILADELPHIA VAROIC

PO BOX 8079

Philadelphia, PA 19101

Phone: 877-294-6380

Also, applications for benefits can be filed directly on the VA website. However, I do not recommend this because you still have to mail in your verification documents that support your application. Thus, I have found that it is better to keep the application and supporting documents altogether. The VA loses paperwork all too often. Your initial efforts in keeping the application with the supporting documentation may help in getting your claim approved faster.

SECRET # 27

You can file your application through the Fast Track System to expedite your claim.

How long does the application and approval process normally take?

If you are filing for a service connected disability, the process generally takes several years (can be up to four years or more).

If you are applying for non-service connected disability benefits, the approval process averages between three to 18 months. Two primary situations affect the duration of the adjudication process:

– How "complete" the application and supporting documents are when submitted and

– Whether the claimant is mentally incapable of managing his own finances, thus, a fiduciary must be appointed. The fiduciary process takes a very long time.

How can you shorten that application process?

First, the VA has implemented a new system to fast track the application process. Essentially, if you have a complete claim that includes all the necessary forms and all the required verification documents, and you don't expect that you'll ever have to add anything else to the file, then you can request that your file be placed on the fast track. To do this, you must file a specific form wherein you waive all of your due process rights.

The due process rights that you are waiving are the scheduled time allowances the VA must otherwise provide to you when responding to VA correspondence and inquiries. As a general rule, as an attorney, I do not like to waive my clients' due process rights and I certainly would not want anyone to do so without first seeking the advice of an attorney. However, in this instance, a claimant can always rescind his or her waiver and elect to go back on the slow track if it is deemed necessary or more desirable.

SECRET # 28

The claimant must personally sign the application form.

Many times our elderly clients have designated a power of attorney agent to manage their affairs for them. The power of attorney agent usually signs all legal documents on behalf of the principal. Thus, when the agent completes the VA application, it is only natural that they would sign the application on behalf of the claimant.

The VA will kick back the application unless it is signed by the applicant personally. The law and VA policy allow an agent to sign the application on behalf of the claimant; however, the adjudicators disregard this permission and delay the application by sending it back and requesting the claimant's signature. The VA does not appear to care whether the claimant is mentally competent to do so or not. But, if the claimant signs an "X", there must be a witness to the signature.

SECRET # 29

The VA will NOT accept privately drafted powers of attorney.

If you have a power of attorney drafted by an attorney or one you drafted yourself, the VA will not accept this. Rather, the VA requires its own "representation" form. The form is VA Form 21-22 (if you use a veteran service organization to help you) or a VA Form 21-22a (if you use a lawyer or family member to help you). No witnesses are required. Only the claimant and the representative must sign it.

The claimant can only have one representative at a time. The VA will only discuss the claim with the representative appointed on the VA Form 21-22.

In many cases, the lawyer assisting with the claim will be the initial representative. Then, when benefits are approved, a new VA Form 21-22a is executed naming a family member as the representative. The new form supersedes the initial form filed with the VA.

The VA will not recognize a formal, court ordered guardianship proceeding either. The VA has its own fiduciary/guardianship process when a person is incapacitated and needs a fiduciary to manage the veteran's income.

SECRET # 30

Do not give the VA original verification documents (i.e. discharge papers, birth certificates, marriage licenses, etc.).

The application process may take longer if you provide only copies of verification materials to the VA; however, if you provide them with originals, they will never give them back to you. Thus, I recommend that you hand deliver your application with all supporting documents to the local VA Regional Office. You can show them the original documents, but provide them with a copy that the VA counselor can certify is a true and correct copy of the original. Or, if you do not live near a regional office, your best alternative is to have the Superior Court in your county of residence, or an accredited VA representative, certify the documents for you. Local veteran service organizations are accredited by the VA and should be able to perform this activity for you.

If you cannot find the military discharge paper (commonly a DD-214), you can order a certified copy from www.archives.gov/veterans/military-service-records/dd-214.html, or you can download Standard Form 180 from that same website and mail in the request. When ordering the discharge papers, you should order at least two certified copies so that you can keep one for yourself.

SECRET # 31

You must submit certified copies of all death certificates or divorce decrees from all prior marriages of both the veteran

and the current spouse.

The VA needs to verify that the veteran is legally married to only one person in order to eliminate the possibility that other claimants may come forward after the veteran's death. Also, the widow of a veteran must verify that she is not legally married to anyone else.

Divorce decrees can be obtained from the Superior Court of the county wherein the divorce occurred. Death certificates can be obtained from the vital statistics department of the state where the person died or was born. If you have difficulty obtaining either of these, the claimant can complete VA Form 21-686c, Declaration of Status of dependents, and have other individuals complete VA Form 21-4170, Supporting Statement Regarding Marriage, to verify the status of all prior and current marriages.

SECRET # 32

The VA is required to expedite an application for benefits if the claimant is receiving Hospice care.

If you have been approved for and are receiving hospice

care, you can submit your physician's orders and a statement from the hospice company to the VA and request that they expedite your claim for benefits.

For years I had the fear that if I told the VA that my client was on hospice, they would delay the adjudication of the claim until after my client died. If the claimant is single with no qualifying individuals who can make a claim for accrued benefits, then the claim died with the claimant and the VA would not pay anything to the estate. Many of my clients feel that the VA deliberately drags its feet for this very purpose.

However, the VA actually has a policy that if a claimant is on hospice, then the VA must expedite the claim through the system. I informed the VA of this with one of my clients who was willing to "see what the VA would do." The VA adjudicator I informed was one that I had built a relationship with, and whom I trusted. He told me to fax the information immediately, which I did. We received an approval notice within two weeks. Now, I cannot guarantee that you will have the same result, but you do need to know the VA has this policy and should follow it when requested to do so by a claimant.

Part IV – Health Care Benefits

The Veterans Health Administration (VHA) is the arm of the VA that administers health care. Programs available for elderly veterans may include inpatient and outpatient care, geriatric evaluations, nursing home care, home health care, adult day care, and respite care.

Before a veteran can get health care from the VA, he or she must "enter" the health care system. Entering the health care system requires that the veteran file a VA Form 1010EZ. The only thing easy about the VA is the name of this form! Truthfully, though, this form is actually easier to complete than many other VA forms. Nevertheless, there are still some traps in the 1010EZ form that an unaware person may not know about. It is very important to read the instructions for the form when filling it out.

You can obtain that form online from the VA website, www4.va.gov/vaforms/, or from a local VA clinic or hospital. Normally at the VA hospital or clinic there is a certain place called "Station 1." This is where you get your veteran health care identification card issued. When you apply for health care benefits, the VA will request that you complete a financial statement form as well. The financial statement form will assist the VA in determining into which priority category you fall.

When you enter the health care system, the VA will assign you to one of eight different priority groups. The priority group to which you are assigned is dependent upon your military service and other factors. For example, priority group one is the highest level priority group. People in this group typically get their services free, without waiting. They are people who have serious injuries due to their military service and who are 100 percent unemployable.

Priority group eight, on the other hand, is at the opposite end of the spectrum. These are veterans who served in the military for a minimum period of time, did not sustain a service connected injury, and have either high net worth or high income. Priority group eight primarily consists of veterans who served in the military, did their time, had an honorable discharge and now want to use their earned benefits.

Whether a veteran has to pay a co-pay for care and

treatment through the VA depends on to which priority group he or she is assigned. If a person refuses to complete the financial statement, he will be charged the highest permissible co-payment. The financial statement form indicates that you don't have to fill it out. But, again, if you don't fill it out, then the VA will assign you the highest applicable co-payment.

After you submit the VA Form 1010EZ, you will have to submit to a physical evaluation by a VA physician. The physical evaluation assists the VA in determining which priority group is appropriate based on your health. For example, a veteran who would normally be in priority group eight may be deemed a priority group four veteran because he needs the assistance of others with his activities of daily living. Priority group four provides more benefits to the veteran than does being in priority group eight.

SECRET # 33

You can continue to use your own doctor.

After enrolling in the system and completing the VA physical examination, the veteran can choose to use VA doctors for ongoing health care needs or can choose to continue using his regular, primary physician. It is not uncommon for me to hear from a client, "We have never applied for the VA health care system because my dad likes his doctors."

Well, I want him to keep using his doctors. But, there are other benefits of being enrolled in the health care system. For example, reduced or free prescriptions, free hearing aids, extended care services, and the list goes on. There are a lot of benefits that a veteran can receive by virtue of being enrolled in the health care system even if that veteran doesn't want or need to use the VA doctors.

VA Nursing Homes

Because long-term care options generally lead to nursing home care at some point, it is essential that you understand what the VA offers.

There are federal VA nursing homes and state VA nursing homes.

For a veteran to be eligible for admission to a federal VA nursing home, the veteran must have a service connected disability rated at 70% or more. Or, the veteran has a service connected disability rating less than 70%, but needs the nursing home level of care due to the service connected disabling condition.

Once admitted to the federal VA nursing home, the cost of care can range from $0-$97 per day. The co-payment is based on the veteran's gross annual income, but not on the veteran's assets. This option is extremely important to know about because it can be a way to preserve precious resources for the veteran, his spouse, and other dependents.

State VA nursing homes are also a wonderful option. Many states have nursing homes that are owned and operated by the state. Because they meet federal VA guidelines, they are subsidized with federal funds.

State VA nursing homes only accept veterans who served in the military during a war-time period. However, to be eligible for care in a state VA home, the veteran does NOT have to have sustained any service connected disabilities. In addition to being a war-time veteran, the veteran must have lived in the state for a particular amount of time before being admitted to the nursing home. Each state has its own laws and policies regarding admission. For example, in Georgia there are two state VA homes, which require that a veteran must have resided in Georgia for five years immediately prior to admission.

State VA homes are generally available to eligible veterans at no cost or a very low cost. In some cases, a slight co-payment is required. In addition, admission and eligibility are not based on income or asset levels. As you can imagine, there may be a waiting list for an available bed.

SECRET # 34

Some private nursing homes — likely in your own community — have federal VA contracts.

Lastly, there is a third option — private nursing homes with a federal VA contract.

These are the nursing homes that you would normally move to in your own community. However, not all private nursing homes have contracts with the VA. Therefore, it is incumbent upon the veteran or family members to research which nursing homes have a contract, and which do not.

To be eligible for admission under the VA contract, the veteran must meet the same eligibility requirements as those pertaining to a federal VA nursing home. Therefore, he must either have a service connected disability rating of 70% or higher, or the reason for the nursing home admission must be due to the service connected disability.

SECRET # 35

Some federal VA nursing homes, and some private nursing homes with a federal VA contract, will admit veterans for care even if the veteran does not meet the service connected disability requirements.

Admission in this case is based on whether the homes have a bed available. Therefore, I recommend you approach the nursing home administrators and ask them what their particular policies are and who they permit to live in their facility.

SECRET # 36

Veterans can obtain their prescriptions from the VA for $9 or less for a 30 day supply.

If a veteran is enrolled in the health care system, he can obtain his prescriptions from the VA clinic. The VA will also mail the prescriptions to the veteran. This is especially helpful for veterans who no longer drive or who do not live close to a VA clinic. The veteran's private physician prescribes the medications and the veteran then submits the prescriptions to the VA to be filled, just as with any other pharmacy.

In many cases, my clients are enrolled in the VA health care system solely to receive the prescription advantage. It is not uncommon to see clients save up to $800 per month on their prescriptions by switching to the VA system. The money my clients save can then be applied to other necessary expenses like home health care, the electric bill, etc.

As with other medical services, the prescription services through the VA are only available to veterans, not dependents. Thus, the spouse or widow of a veteran cannot obtain prescriptions from the VA unless she, herself, is a veteran.

SECRET # 37

Elderly veterans can receive Extended Care Services from the VA which can delay the premature need to move to an assisted living or nursing home environment.

A benefit through the health care system that many veterans do not know about, or know how to obtain, is called the extended care services program. This program is available for veterans who are enrolled in the health care system. Usually, the veteran lives at home and needs additional care.

The extended care services program can provide assistance with companion care in the home, provide respite care to give the regular caregiver some time off, pay for the cost of adult day care programs, and more.

The extended care services program and the available services are state specific. This means that each state may have different services or no services. The reason for this is that the VA does not actually provide the service; rather, the VA contracts with local vendors. The resulting benefit to the veteran is that he or she can use these services at a reduced rate, or for free depending on which priority level the veteran has been assigned by the VA. The maximum co-payment on any of the services listed above is generally much less than what the veteran would normally have to pay privately for the same exact service from the same or a comparable company. The true benefit is being able to stay home and receive the necessary service at a discounted rate or for free.

I'll give you one example. Juliette, the wife of Robert, a veteran, came to see me to discuss the VA improved pension with aid and attendance benefits. Robert had Parkinson's and Alzheimer's disease and was not safe staying at home alone. Juliette still worked part-time at a job she really enjoyed. Her main desire was to keep Robert at home as long as possible. He could still walk unassisted, dress himself, feed himself, and do the regular activities of daily living without any help. However, Robert was a fall risk and sometimes would leave the house and forget how to get back home. He needed supervision to remain safe from the harms of his environment. When Juliette was exploring assisted living facilities, she heard about the VA pension. She thought this would be an ideal solution to obtain additional income to pay for home health care.

Juliette and Robert had too many assets to qualify for the pension benefit. In fact, they had a second home that was worth around $900,000. Because the home had been in the family for generations, they did not want to sell it. Moreover, if they sold the home, they would incur a huge tax liability. Other than the second home, which is a countable resource for VA pension purposes, Juliette and Robert had very modest assets and income.

Instead of relying on the VA pension, which is what Juliette came to me about, I told her about the extended care services program, which would allow her husband to get assistance with home health care. The maximum co-pay in their situation was $97 per day because of their combined income and assets, which made Robert a priority 8. Twenty-four hour home care can cost $12,000 or more per month. But with the extended care services program, Robert would not have to pay more than approximately $2,910 per month for the same care. This was definitely more affordable and allowed Robert to stay at home.

To apply for extended care services, the veteran must be enrolled in the VA health care system. Enrollment in both programs may be done simultaneously. Use VA Form 1010EC to apply for the extended care services program.

SECRET # 38

Only Veterans can access the VA health care system. Spouses and other dependents (with very few exceptions) cannot use the VA health care system.

Part V – Burial Benefits

SECRET # 39

Veterans and their spouses can be buried at a national cemetery at no cost.

There is a national cemetery system wherein burial benefits are available to veterans. The benefits can include a grave site in any of the 125 national cemeteries as long as there is available space, the opening and closing of the grave, perpetual care, a government headstone or marker, a burial flag, and a Presidential memorial certificate. Cremated remains may also be buried in national cemeteries in the same manner and with the same honors as casket burials.

Widows of veterans may also be eligible for burial allowances as reimbursement for out-of-pocket expenses.

Spouses and dependents of veterans, whether they die before or after the veteran, can also be buried in a national cemetery. The benefit includes burial in the veteran's plot, perpetual care, and the spouse or dependent's name, date of birth, and death inscribed on the veteran's headstone at no cost to the family. You may be wondering "what if the spouse dies before the veteran, do they have to wait until the veteran dies before they can be buried at the national cemetery, or can the spouse be buried first?"

If the non-veteran spouse dies first, the spouse can be buried in the veteran's space and when the veteran dies, he will be buried there also.

Private Cemetery System

Other than the 125 national cemeteries, there is also a private cemetery system. Burial benefits available for veterans buried in the private burial system include a government headstone or marker, a burial flag and a Presidential memorial certificate. This is also at no cost to the family.

However, spouses and dependents are not eligible for any benefits in a private cemetery.

To apply for the burial allowance related to a veteran's death, file VA Form 21-530.

To request a military headstone or marker to place on a grave site in a private, non-military cemetery, file VA Form 40-1330.

To determine whether you are eligible for burial in a national cemetery, please call a Veteran's Benefits Counselor at 1-800-827-1000. Eligibility is based on many factors, which can be found at:

www.cem.va.gov/cem/bbene/eligible.asp.

SECRET # 40

You must have the military discharge papers in hand in order to be buried at a military cemetery.

One of the most important things to do is to obtain a copy of the veteran's military discharge BEFORE death and keep it close at hand in a safe place. Otherwise, burial may be delayed or denied.

Part VI – Getting Help

Who can help veterans obtain the benefits they have earned, need, and deserve? You would think that anyone who has the requisite knowledge could help you. That is not true.

SECRET # 41

There is a very specific, yet limited, list of the types of people who can assist a veteran with the preparation, presentation, and prosecution of a claim.

A. Veterans can go through the process without any help.

Veterans are not required to have a representative to assist them with their claims or appeals. In fact, most veterans try to navigate the process on their own. But, when you feel you want the assistance of a trained professional, help is available.

B. Veteran Service Organizations can help.

Veteran service organizations (VSO) are approved non-profit organizations that have been accredited by the VA to represent veterans with their claims. Examples of VSOs include the American Red Cross, the American Legion, Disabled American Veterans, Veterans of Foreign Wars, and many others. Oftentimes VSOs will have offices at the local VA Regional Office where you file your original claim.

In addition to traditional VSOs, each state has multiple state VA offices that are sanctioned by the Governor of that state. They operate just like a VSO, but are funded by the state.

C. Individuals Accredited by the VA.

Individuals who are accredited by the VA can also represent claimants. These are usually non-lawyers, and not people working for a VSO. To be accredited by the VA, a non-lawyer must take and pass a test administered by the VA. The current test has 25 multiple choice/true-false questions.

D. A One-time Power of Attorney Agent.

A one-time power of attorney agent does NOT have

to be accredited by the VA. This is traditionally a claimant's family member, such as a spouse or child. It can also be a friend, neighbor, or anyone who knows the veteran's circumstances and is willing to help.

In this situation, the relative or friend would become the claimant's representative by having the claimant sign VA Form 21-22a that was discussed previously in Secret # 29.

One question always comes up when I discuss the one-time power of attorney agent option. "What if a daughter helps her father file a claim; he later dies and now the daughter wants to help the surviving spouse file a claim; can she do that even thought that would be TWO times?"

Yes, the daughter can still help the mother with her claim. What the VA is trying to prevent with the one-time power of attorney option, is having a neighbor, for example, helping the entire neighborhood or making a business out of it.

E. Attorneys who are accredited by the VA can help

veterans.

Not just any attorney can assist a veteran with the preparation, presentation, and prosecution of a claim. The attorney must be accredited by the VA. Attorneys do not have to take a test, but they must submit an application to the VA and be approved by them before they can legally assist veterans with their claims. This became a requirement as of June 23, 2008.

To find out if an attorney in your area is accredited, you can search the VA website at the following link: www4.va.gov/ogc/apps/accreditation/index.html. At this link you can type in the name of the individual you are inquiring about and it will tell you if he or she is accredited. You may also type in your state and the site will list all accredited attorneys or agents in that state.

Part VII – Attorneys' Fees

You may try the VA process on your own because you believe attorneys are expensive. However, you may be surprised to learn that attorneys cannot charge for certain assistance.

SECRET # 42

No private or non-profit organization, nor individual, including lawyers, can charge for the preparation, presentation and prosecution of a claim.

If you are eligible for and seeking VA benefits, it is illegal for anyone to charge you to assist with preparing the application for benefits, for filing it on your behalf, and for following up on its status. If someone charges to help you in completing your application for benefits, then you should report them to your local VA regional office.

SECRET # 43

Once a veteran's claim is denied or approved for fewer benefits than the claimant was seeking, the veteran can hire a paid representative to assist with the appeal AFTER a Notice of Disagreement has been filed with the VA.

The Notice of Disagreement (NOD) is the first indication from a veteran to the VA that the veteran disagrees with the VA's decision. It is not yet the formal appeal, but it is the first indication of "I don't like the decision and I plan to appeal unless you change it." The attorney CANNOT charge to assist the veteran with drafting the NOD.

It is only after the NOD has been filed with the VA that the attorney can then step in and say, "Would you like some help? I'm going to charge you to assist with the appeal." And the veteran can say, "I would love some help with my appeal and I would love to pay you to advocate on my behalf against the VA."

SECRET # 44

A Notice of Disagreement filed BEFORE June 20, 2007, has different rules.

For veterans who filed appeals (NODs) prior to June 20, 2007, but still need representation through the system, an attorney can help them, but cannot charge for that representation until the veteran has received a final disposition from the Board of Veterans Appeals (BVA).

For older appeals initiated prior to June 20, 2007, most veterans use a veteran service organization to help them with the appeal process up through the BVA level. However, after receiving a denial from the BVA (which the majority of veterans do), veterans seek private legal counsel.

How Much Can Lawyers Charge You?

For assistance with your appeal, a lawyer must have a written legal agreement signed by both of you. The agreement must detail the services provided and the terms. The agreement must then be provided to the VA for approval. The VA will determine whether the legal fee being charged is reasonable.

SECRET # 45

The fee is presumed to be reasonable if the attorney charges no more than 20% of what you receive in past due benefits.

For example, if you are seeking benefits to begin January 1, 2008; received a denial on June 5, 2008; hired a lawyer in August of 2008 (after you filed your notice of disagreement); and the VA finally awards you benefits in July of 2009, which are retroactive to January 1, 2008, a lawyer's fee of 20% of all benefits received from January 1, 2008, through the date of approval would be considered reasonable by the VA.

The fee is not limited to 20% of past due benefits, however. Many attorneys will charge up to one-third of past-due benefits. While this is not presumed to be reasonable by the VA, the VA will in most cases approve this fee arrangement if the lawyer can prove that the case is one that requires a lot of work, special knowledge, and is difficult in nature.

A lawyer may also charge an hourly rate or a flat fee, as long as the VA approves the arrangement. The reason the VA requires that attorneys send their legal services agreements in for approval is to ensure attorneys are not financially exploiting or gouging veterans.

Fees for Elder Care Planning and Veterans' Benefits Planning for Seniors

SECRET # 46

Elder Care and Estate Planning Attorneys are allowed to charge clients for the elder care and estate planning work they do for veterans.

Most elder care and estate planning attorneys do not assist veterans with service connected disability appeals or any other type of appeals. Rather, they focus their services on assisting clients in preserving their independence, assets, and quality of life. To reach those goals, the attorney must devise an individual plan for the client that includes a variety of different strategies. **The attorney CAN charge a fee for this specialized service and knowledge.**

Elder care attorneys need to know about health care issues, long-term care options, veterans' benefits eligibility rules, and Medicaid laws. A general practitioner, real estate lawyer, family law attorney, etc., is not usually equipped with the knowledge or education to understand how all of the different issues and benefits programs work together. Keep in mind, if an attorney is providing you advice on qualifying for VA benefits beyond just general information, the attorney must be accredited by the VA. Additionally, any work the attorney does for you that involves preparing and filing the actual VA application must be performed for free.

Part VIII – Resources for You

SECRET # 47

Knowing about reliable resources where you can obtain credible information is the key to obtaining the Veterans' Benefits you have earned!

1. **Department of Veterans Affairs:** www.va.gov

2. **VA Forms:** www.vba.va.gov/pubs/forms1.htm

3. **M21-1 and M21-1MR,** Adjudication Manual; www.warms.vba.gov/m21_1.html; www.warms.vba.va.gov/M21_1MR.html

4. **Veterans Benefits Manual,** published by LexisNexis

5. **VisPro,** software to streamline the application process; created by Veterans Information Services, Inc. and co-authored by Victoria L. Collier, Attorney; www.info4vets.com (currently only available for sale to professionals and organizations, not individuals)

6. **National Organization of Veterans Advocates** (NOVA): www.vetadvocates.com

7. **National Veterans Legal Services Program:**
www.nvlsp.com

8. **Veterans Advocates Group of America:**
www.vagamembers.com

9. **VA blogs and listserves**

   A. www.vawatchdog.org

   B. www.veteranaid.org/

Victoria Collier enlisted in the U.S. Air Force at the age of 19. She served on active duty from 1989 – 1995, during the Gulf War (Desert Storm). Her first trained skill was as a carpenter/mason. She then cross-trained to become a paralegal. After leaving the military in 1995, Victoria finished her undergraduate degree in psychology at Valdosta State University, and then pursued a *Juris Doctorate* at the University of Nebraska-Lincoln. Victoria established The Elder & Disability Law Firm of Victoria L. Collier, PC in 2002. From 2001-2004, she was a 1st Lieutenant in the U.S. Army Reserves, JAG Corps.

Victoria is a member of:

United States Supreme Court, admitted 2009

United States Court of Appeals for Veterans Claims, admitted 2007

Appointed by Georgia Governor Purdue to the Council on Aging, Advisory Board, 2010

State Bar of Georgia, Elder Law Section, Chair 2010, VC 2007-2009

Atlanta Bar Association, Elder Law Committee, Chair 2004-2005, Vice Chair 2003-2004

National Academy of Elder Law Attorneys (NAELA), Member since 2002

NAELA, Georgia Chapter, Chair 2008-2009

National Organization of Veteran Advocates, Member

Veterans Advocates Group of America, Co-Founder

Georgia Super Lawyers, Rising Star in 2005, 2009

Ms. Collier is an entrepreneur and has created the following successful businesses:

- The Elder & Disability Law Firm of Victoria L. Collier, PC

- Trust Associates, Inc., co-founder

- Veterans Advocate Group of Am   ca, co-founder

- Collier Communications, LLC

- The Collier Building, LLC

- Trail Creek Properties, LLC, co-founder

- Getting to Baby, LLC, co-founder

Ms. Collier is a motivational speaker for business organizations and military groups.

To inquire about her availability, you can contact her at:
Victoria L. Collier, Attorney
160 Clairemont Ave, Ste 440
Decatur, GA 30030

404-370-0696 / 404-370-0697 fax
1-866-371-6100
www.elderlawgeorgia.com

This book is available for purchase (as a single copy and specially priced 10-packs) at www.elderlawgeorgia.com. Please contact the office above for larger bulk purchases.